JUN 1 9 2004

INTERNATIONAL FALLS PUBLIC LIBRARY
750 4th Street
INTERNATIONAL FALLS, MN 56649

U.S. ARMY

FIGHTING FORCES

JASON COOPER

Rourke
Publishing LLC
Vero Beach, Florida 32964

© 2004 Rourke Publishing LLC

All rights reserved. No part of this book may be reproduced or utilized in any form or by any means, electronic or mechanical including photocopying, recording, or by any information storage and retrieval system without permission in writing from the publisher.

www.rourkepublishing.com

PHOTO CREDITS: Title page, pp. 5, 13, 19, 20, 22 courtesy of Defense Visual Information Center; pp. 6, 9, 11, 25, 27 courtesy of National Archives; p.14 courtesy of Army Special Operations Command; p. 29 courtesy of U.S. Air Force

Title page: *An infantryman uses a rope to leave a UH-1 Iroquois helicopter.*

Editor: Frank Sloan

Cover and page design by Nicola Stratford

Library of Congress Cataloging-in-Publication Data

Cooper, Jason, 1942-
 U.S. Army / Jason Cooper.
   v. cm. — (Fighting forces)
Includes bibliographical references and index.
Contents: Defending the United States — The U.S. Army at work — The Army Command — Life in the Army — Army weapons — The Army's Beginnings.
  ISBN 1-58952-713-5 (hardcover)
 1. United States. Army—Juvenile literature. [1. United States. Army.] I. Title. II. Series: Cooper, Jason, 1942- Fighting Forces.

 UA23.C67218 2003
 355'.00973—dc21

2003005284

Printed in the USA

CG/CG

Table of Contents

Chapter 1 Defending the United States 4

Chapter 2 The U.S. Army at Work 8

Chapter 3 The Army Command 10

Chapter 4 Life in the Army 12

Chapter 5 Army Weapons 18

Chapter 6 The Army's Beginnings 24

Glossary 30

Index 32

Further Reading 32

Website to Visit 32

Defending the United States

CHAPTER ONE

The U.S. Army's job is to defend the United States and her interests on land. The Army is the largest and oldest of the nation's **armed services**. It has about 480,000 men and women on active duty. It has more than half a million soldiers in the **reserve** and in the **National Guard**. The Army also has more than 200,000 **civilian** workers. Civilians are not enlisted members of the Army.

Army troops and tanks help defend America and her interests. ▶

The U.S. Army is not the biggest of the world's armies. But it is highly trained and skilled. And it is equipped with the world's most modern equipment and weapons. Army units can be sent quickly to anywhere in the world to act with force or as keepers of the peace.

The United States has Army soldiers at **bases** in western Europe, Japan, South Korea, parts of Latin America, and elsewhere.

Army soldiers provide a service to their country. Life in the army can be an adventure and a wonderful learning experience. It can also be dangerous. Hundreds of thousands of soldiers have died defending the United States and its allies.

ARMY FORCES	
CORPS	TWO OR MORE DIVISIONS
DIVISION	10,000 - 18,000 SOLDIERS
BRIGADE	3,000 - 4,000 SOLDIERS
BATTALION	500-800 SOLDIERS
COMPANY	100-200 SOLDIERS
BATTERY	ARTILLERY GROUP
CAVALRY	HIGHLY MOBILE FORCE

◀ *The Army has had many thousands of heroes who did their jobs despite great danger. Here two World War II infantrymen take shelter by a tank during a break in the fighting in Geich, Germany, in December, 1944.*

The U.S. Army at Work

CHAPTER TWO

The Army never wants war. But the Army's job is to be prepared to use force if it must. If an enemy threatens, the Army and other armed services can rush to the nation's defense.

In peacetime, the Army can be called upon to assist the victims of major floods, fires, and storms. In addition, the Army does public works through its Army Corps of Engineers. These include **dredging** and building dams and canals for flood control.

ARMY FORCES

The U.S. Army sometimes trains the armed services of other nations. It also supplies military equipment, such as tanks, to other nations.

▲ A section of Charleston, South Carolina, lies in ruin after Americans fought Americans during the Civil War.

9

CHAPTER THREE

The Army Command

Soldiers in the Army take orders from officers, like lieutenants, majors, or generals. But officers take orders, too. Some officers have a higher **rank** than other officers. High-ranking officers give orders to lower-ranking officers.

Even the Army's highest ranking officers, though, take orders. The Army's number one commander is a civilian, the president of the United States. The president is the commander-in-chief of all the armed forces. When the most important military decisions have to be made, the president makes them.

Highest ranks in descending order

General
Lieutenant General
Major General
Brigadier General
Colonel
Lieutenant Colonel
Major
Captain
First Lieutenant
Second Lieutenant

American soldiers invaded France on D-Day, June 6, 1944. General Dwight D. Eisenhower (left) gave the order of the day to American paratroopers: "Full victory—nothing else."

The Army also has other civilian bosses. One is the secretary of the Army. The secretary of the Army is the chief of the Department of the Army. That department is part of the U.S. government's Department of Defense. The Army, Navy, Air Force, and Marine Corps are all managed by the Department of Defense. The secretary of Defense is the secretary of the Army's boss.

Life in the Army

The Army is made up of volunteers. No one has to join the Army or any other American armed service. The armed services **recruit** men and women to join them.

Men and women between the ages of 17 and 35 can enlist in the Army. They must be able to pass the Army's physical and written tests. A person can enlist in the Army for a term of two to six years. Some people who enlist in the Army make **careers** of their work.

Recruits can continue Army school to learn very special skills, like flying helicopters.

▲ An Army Special Forces (Green Berets) officer watches an action drill with his men.

Recruits undergo basic training at an Army training base. They learn skills, such as how to march and how to handle weapons. They learn first aid, the use of a compass, and **combat** skills. They learn Army discipline and how to work together as a team.

A few Army soldiers belong to Special Operations units. Each of these groups is specially trained and highly skilled. The Army Rangers, for example, are trained in nighttime attack.

The Army's Special Forces, often called the Green Berets, are outstanding fighters and foreign language specialists. The Army has several other Special Operations Groups.

Army soldiers have several paths to becoming officers. About three of every four Army officers began their careers in Army ROTC (Reserve Officer Training Corps). One of them is Colin Powell. He was a general before becoming the U.S. secretary of State in 2001.

FACT FILE

After several weeks of basic training, most recruits attend an Army school. There they learn to become expert at one or more of some 600 Army skills.

The Army also trains officers at the United States Military Academy at West Point, New York. The U.S. Military Academy is the oldest of the service academies. It was founded in 1802. Many of America's most famous military officers went to West Point. Among them were Dwight D. Eisenhower, Ulysses S. Grant, Robert E. Lee, Stonewall Jackson, Douglas MacArthur, George Patton, and George Armstrong Custer.

 Army Weapons

CHAPTER FIVE

The U.S. Army's weapons range from aircraft and guided missiles to hand grenades and rifles. The Army is also equipped with machine guns, **mortars**, tanks, flame throwers, and big, cannon-like guns.

The Army has several different groups that are prepared to fight enemy forces. The largest of the Army groups is the **infantry**. Infantry soldiers generally fight on their feet. They may enter a battle, however, by other means, such as parachute or helicopter.

▲ A soldier equipped with night vision goggles aims a grenade launcher. The launcher has an infrared aiming light to work in darkness.

Army **artillery** units fire big guns onto enemy positions. Artillery guns are often used before the infantry or **armored** units attack. The Army's **howitzers** fire shells as far as 13 miles (21 kilometers). Other rocket-fired artillery weapons can fire shells even further.

The Army's fighting vehicles make up its armored groups. The best-known armored vehicles are tanks. The Army's heavily armed and extremely fast Abrams tank was an important fighting vehicle in Iraq in 2003. The Abrams can travel up to 55 miles (88 kilometers) per hour. It can fire on the move, even from rough, rocky surfaces.

Another important Army vehicle is the Bradley fighting vehicle, described as a "taxi in armor." Bradleys haul soldiers forward to work in tandem with tank operations.

◀ *An infantryman launches a Stinger missile.*

▲ *An Apache Longbow helicopter whirls over Texas during a training flight.*

The Army does not fly high-powered attack jets. But it does have aircraft to aid its overall missions. Army planes are used for many purposes. Big transport planes are used to haul Army soldiers from place to place. Other planes are used to spy on enemy positions and take photos from the air. Spotter planes find enemy positions and tell artillery units where to aim.

The Army's missile units have many kinds of ground-to-air and ground-to-ground missiles. The Pershing II missile, for example, is a long-range ground-to-ground missile. It is fired from a ground support at a ground target up to 1,100 miles (1,760 kilometers) away.

FACT FILE ★

Army helicopters are also used for several purposes. They may scout ahead of ground forces or haul soldiers and equipment. Some helicopters have built-in guns.

THE ARMY'S BEGINNINGS

CHAPTER SIX

Each American colony had its own little army in 1775. As the Revolutionary War (1775-1783) with England became likely, the colonies made a decision. They would build an army with men from all the colonies. On June 14, 1775, the Continental Congress acted to create the Continental Army. That was the beginning of the United States Army. Of course, until the colonies pushed British soldiers off American soil there would be no United States.

The first mission of General George Washington's ragged little army seemed impossible. But Washington and his men did the impossible. The British left America in defeat. The colonies would have a new army, the United States Army.

An old painting shows General George Washington on his horse during his army's retreat to Long Island, New York, in 1776. ▶

The American Army rebuilt some of its strength and size in a second war against the British (1812-1815). It later fought Mexico (1846-1848). That was the first time American soldiers had been sent into land battle outside the country.

> **FACT FILE** ★
>
> THE ARMY HAS HAD MANY TESTS IN THE MORE THAN 200 YEARS SINCE WASHINGTON DEFEATED THE BRITISH. WASHINGTON MAY HAVE HAD AS MANY AS 30,000 SOLDIERS. BUT BY THE LATE 1780S THE NEW NATION HAD FEWER THAN 1,000.

The nation split in two when Southern states tried to create their own nation in 1861. President Abraham Lincoln and Congress would not permit a breakup of the country. The Civil War (1861-1865) followed. Both Northern and Southern armies grew. The armies fought huge, bloody battles at such places as Shiloh, Gettysburg, Antietam, Richmond, Atlanta, Fredericksburg, and Bull Run.

During that time, army warfare began to change. The railroad was widely used. The telegraph became important. The Army used observation balloons. The first machine guns and repeating rifles were brought to the battlefields. Artillery became more accurate and more deadly.

Union soldiers of the 1st Connecticut Heavy Artillery stand by their mortars. These artillery weapons fired at Confederate troops defending Yorktown, Virginia, in April, 1862. ▶

By the end of the Civil War, the Union Army had about one million men in uniform. But it soon trimmed down to 25,000. This is the Army that fought American Indians. By 1886, the Indian Wars were over, but the Army faced new challenges. The Army fought in the Spanish-American War (1898). In 1917 and 1918 the U.S. Army helped the English and French armies defeat Germany in World War I (1914-1918).

America was not fully prepared for another war in Europe. When World War II (1939-1945) began, the American Army had just 190,000 soldiers. But by 1945 it had more than 8 million! Army troops fought in both the Atlantic and Pacific areas of the war.

The Army was downsized after World War II. In 1950 it began growing again when North Korea attacked South Korea. It grew to more than one and one-half million American soldiers. The Korean War ended in 1953.

The Vietnam War (1957-1975) was the American Army's longest war. The United States hoped to stop North Vietnam from taking over South Vietnam. America sent very few soldiers to Vietnam at first. But by 1969, more than 350,000 Army soldiers were in the country. In 1973 the United States pulled its armed forces from Vietnam. North Vietnam then took over the South, making North and South Vietnam a single nation in 1975.

The modern U.S. Army is **mobile**, powerful, and highly trained. It continues to help keep peace while remaining always battle ready.

The U.S. Army was again in action during the Persian Gulf War against Iraq in February, 1991. The Army helped bring about a quick and complete victory. Army troops were also sent into combat against Afghanistan in 2001 and against Iraq in 2003.

▲ *Modern-day Army airborne troops land during a training exercise. The men jumped from Air Force C-141 Starlifter airplanes.*

Glossary

armed services (AHRMED SUR vuh sez) — the military forces of a government, such as the U.S. Army

armored (AHRM ered) — covered by steel for protection

artillery (AHR till er ee) — those weapons and forces that fire explosives a long distance from the ground

bases (BAY suz) — centers or headquarters for military units

careers (KUH reerz) — long-term jobs or long periods of working at one's chosen job

civilian (suh VIL yun) — one who is not a member of the armed forces

combat (CAHM bat) — warfare; fighting with violence

dredging (DREDJ ing) — digging out mud or other material from a waterway

howitzers (HOW it zuhrz) — short cannons that fire explosives; types of artillery weapons

infantry (IN fun tree) — soldiers on the ground; foot soldiers

military (MIL uh tair ee) — having to do with or being part of a nation's armed forces

mobile (MOH buhl) — able to move easily from place to place

mortars (MOR tuhrz) — firing devices, such as cannons

National Guard (NASH uh nul GARD) — the branch of the Army that may be active in helping with national emergencies at home or out of the country

rank (RANK) — a level of command or authority

recruit (REE kroot) (verb) — to urge one to join a group, such as a military service

recruits (REE krootz) (noun) — those who join a military service

reserve (REE SURV) — non-active soldiers who may be called to active duty in a national emergency

INDEX

aircraft 18, 23
armed services 4
Army Corps of
 Engineers 8
Army Rangers 15
artillery 21
bases 7
careers 12
Civil War 26, 27
Department of Defense 11
dredging 8
Green Berets 15
helicopters 23
howitzers 21
infantry 18
Korean War 28
missiles 18, 21, 23
recruits 15
Revolutionary War 24
Special Operations 15
tanks 21
Vietnam War 28
weapons 5, 15, 18
West Point 17
World War I 27
World War II 28

FURTHER READING

Doughtery, Terri and Thomas Evelyn. *The U.S. Army at War*. Capstone, 2001
Gartman, Gene. *Life in Army Basic Training*. Children's Press, 2000
Sawyer, Susan. *The Army in Action*. Enslow, 2001

WEBSITE TO VISIT

www.army.mil

ABOUT THE AUTHOR

Jason Cooper has written several children's books about a variety of topics for Rourke Publishing, including the recent series *Eye to Eye with Big Cats.*

INTERNATIONAL FALLS PUBLIC LIBRARY
750 4th Street
INTERNATIONAL FALLS, MN 56649